DORA DINOSAUR

Written by Anthony Robinson
Illustrated by Aleksei Bitskoff

Dora was a rather small dinosaur.

Her friend Paul was a dodo.

He was even smaller.

They lived long ago in a land far away called Home.

They liked chasing creepy-crawlies and floating rafts on the river.

One autumn dawn they met
at the ford.
Dora saw Paul first and
jumped out!

"Let's hit some targets," said Paul.
They gathered some stones and
jumped onto the raft.

"Look, a target! Can you hit that tall tree?" asked Dora.

"Good shot," said Dora.
Then an awful scream burst
through the air.

"You hit a stegosaurus!" cried Dora.
"Quick! Let's scarper!" said Paul.

"Can a stegosaurus swim?"
asked Dora.

"I hope not!" said Paul as they
turned the bend.

They hauled the raft out of the river.

"I am hungry," said Paul.

Dora saw some plums and clawed down a few.

Dora started to take a big bite.

Suddenly there was a small squeak.

"Don't eat me!" blurted a bug.

"But I like bugs," slurped Dora.
The bug shivered.

"Who are you?" asked Paul.

"I am Bug," said the bug.

"I am lost and all alone."

"I want to go home, but I can't," said Bug.

"Dozy Bug, **this** is Home!" cried Dora. "Home at last," said Bug, and he yawned happily.